T0046962

Mathematics
in the School Grounds

Learning through Landscapes

— ZOE RHYDDERCH-EVANS —

**Learning through
LANDSCAPES**

The Learning Through Landscapes Trust aims to heighten
the awareness of Local Education Authority officers, school
governors, parents, heads and teachers in schools, of the
teaching and learning potential which exists in the school
landscape. It seeks to stimulate changes in the quality and
use of the land surrounding schools, to encourage the
better use of existing resources for learning and to improve
the environment within which learning takes place.

For further details, please contact:

The Information and Publicity Officer
Learning through Landscapes Trust
Third Floor
Southside Offices
The Law Courts
Winchester
Hants
SO23 9DL

Tel: (0962) 846258

SOUTHGATE

Copyright © Zoe Rhydderch-Evans, 1993
Copyright © Illustrations Southgate Publishers Ltd, 1993

First published 1993 by Southgate Publishers Ltd
Reprinted 1996, 1998, 2001

Southgate Publishers Ltd
The Square, Sandford, Crediton, Devon EX17 4LW

All rights reserved. Parts of this book may be photocopied
by the purchaser or the purchaser's school/organization for
use within that school/organization only.

Printed and bound in Great Britain by Short Run Press,
Exeter, Devon.

British Library Cataloguing in Publication Data
A CIP catalogue record for this book is available from the
British Library.

ISBN 1-85741-021-1

Contents

ACKNOWLEDGMENTS

I appreciate enormously the privilege of working alongside the staff of Cowick First School. Any individual work that I produce is only possible because of the professional stimulation and encouragement that I receive from being a member of this team.

Sally Dyer, the Deputy Head of the school, has made a very significant contribution to this book by preparing all the tables of activities. She has given me many ideas and helped me to develop others.

I must also single out for special thanks: Elizabeth Chadwick, a far better mathematician than I could ever hope to be, and Beverley Valentine and Pippa Moodie whose ever positive response to the words 'could you just' cheers the heart and makes all things possible.

I would also like to record the following major influences:

The National Curriculum Mathematics working group reports which totally support all efforts made by primary teachers to make their mathematics teaching lively and developmentally appropriate.

The teachers, lecturers, advisers and inspectors I have met through inservice courses in many parts of England and Wales. They have shared their own enthusiasms with me and challenged and honed my thinking about children learning mathematics.

The cover photograph and a number of the photographs inside the book were taken at Pilgrim Primary School, Plymouth. Other photographs, taken at Cowick First School, are by the author. Photographs on p.20 are: top © Learning through Landscapes/ Coombes Infants School; bottom © Learning through Landscapes.

The extracts on p.6 are taken from the Interim Report of the Mathematics Working Group, and are reproduced by permission of the Controller of Her Majesty's Stationery Office.

Introduction

School grounds can provide a stimulus for a wide range of mathematical investigations and activities. This book contains suggestions for activities which fulfil requirements for National Curriculum Programmes of Study in Mathematics. The structure of the book follows the organization of the Mathematics Attainment Targets, with the exception of the Measurement section. There are also references to other cross-curricular activities relating to Science, Technology, English, P.E., Geography and Economic Awareness.

The book is divided into four sections reflecting the main areas of Mathematics taught in primary schools – Number, Measurement, Shape and Space, and Data Work. In each section, possible approaches to this work in the school grounds are outlined, and examples given, followed by tables of activities for Key Stage 1 and Key Stage 2 which relate particular areas of the school grounds to the mathematical skills and concepts. Suggestions are provided for activities arising from Buildings, Pathways and Visitors, Allotments, Trees and Shrubs, Conservation Area, Pond, Animals, Games and Activities, and Weather.

At the end of each section there are some photocopiable (pupil) worksheets. These have been designed for use in school grounds, but have a wider application as well. It is hoped that some of them may also be used in pupils' gardens, nearby parks, open spaces on walks, on school trips or at field study centres. The worksheets are intended primarily for Key Stage 2 pupils, but they can easily be adapted and used as verbal instructions for Key Stage 1 pupils.

Many of the activities can be attempted immediately, even by those with only the most basic school grounds provision, such as tarmac, grassed areas and a few flower-beds. A richer and more diverse range of activities can occur where school grounds development has taken place. As a result of the burgeoning interest in the environment over the past ten years, many schools have developed their grounds to include ponds, wild areas, butterfly gardens, bird-feeding stations, tree nurseries and wooded areas. The Learning Through Landscapes Trust has shown how effective such features can be when used for a wide range of formal and informal curriculum activities.

If your school grounds provision is limited, some of these activities can be undertaken in close proximity to the school in local parks or open spaces. Alternatively, while beginning on some activities straight away, plans could be put in motion for making environmental changes in your own grounds for future use.

The Learning Through Landscapes Trust's research has shown that sustainable school grounds developments occur when you:

- Take a holistic long-term view about what is possible.

- Use children's ideas in your planning sessions.

- Involve children and the school community from the start.

- Involve parents in fund-raising and changes made.

- See the grounds as part of the local community rather than the exclusive property of the school.

To help schools manage the process of changing their grounds, Learning through Landscapes has produced a number of useful resources. The 'Survey' and 'Getting Started' packs in the Esso Schoolwatch series are of particular interest for teachers and pupils (see Bibliography).

Individual teachers will want to select activities which fit the developmental needs of their individual pupils. Consultation with pupils before, during and after these activities is essential!

Teachers can help children select the most

appropriate means of communicating and recording their mathematics – orally, in small groups, by talk-on-tape, diagrams, pictures, annotated drawings, formal handwritten accounts, graphs, models and charts or using a word processor or computer.

The detailed suggestions for activities in this book are intended to be used by teachers who can introduce each activity in a problem-solving manner: How can we measure ...? Can we ...? How can we find out ...? and so on.

When your children are undertaking school grounds investigations for National Curriculum mathematical activities, it is inevitable that other areas of the curriculum will be involved. New language and vocabulary work takes place, factual reporting and record-keeping, descriptive and interpretive writing, research, discussion and summarizing. School grounds work affords many opportunities for the use of combined Maths, Science and Technology as well as environmental issues and Geography.

The National Curriculum and Mathematics in the School Grounds

The Mathematics Working Group had some very powerful things to say in their Interim Report published in Autumn 1987 on how mathematics is learned. They developed this wisdom in the August 1988 proposals. It seems to be of the utmost importance if we are to do right by our pupils and by the working party that our teaching should be weighted towards the Programmes of Study and the development of a positive attitude towards the subject of mathematics.

In paragraph 2.3 of the Interim Report the working party state that the National Curriculum should encourage:

- Motivation and interest in the subject.

- Pleasure and enjoyment from mathematical activities.

- Appreciation of the purpose, power and relevance of mathematics.

- Perseverance in tackling an extended task.

- Independence of thought.

- Confidence to do mathematics at an appropriate level.

- Satisfaction from achievement.

In paragraph 2.4 further requirements are suggested:

- More practical problem solving and investigational work which is relevant to the pupils so that the importance of mathematics can be better understood.

- Ample scope for schools to make the learning experiences interesting and enjoyable.

- The encouragement of creativity and inventiveness, and recognition of the lasting effect of pupils finding their own ways of doing things.

- Opportunities to use mathematics across the curriculum at all stages of education.

- The use of calculators and microcomputers as appropriate.

- More co-operative problem solving.

- A reduction in the uncomprehending manipulation of symbols.

- Encouragement to pupils to communicate and discuss mathematical ideas.

If this book is successful, readers will see how the school grounds can be used to help to deliver the National Curriculum Programmes of Study in the way that the working group intended. Primary teachers are by now so familiar with the Mathematics Attainment Targets that they will easily recognize all the intended links and networks and will go on to exploit them in ways that are appropriate for 'their' pupils in 'their' grounds.

Why teach Mathematics outside?

Children need to be taught to appreciate Mathematics as a discipline in its own right and also to understand that they will need mathematical knowledge and skills to help them solve problems or communicate with precision almost every day of their lives. In addition to lessons which concentrate on mathematics alone, they will also need to learn that mathematical knowledge, understanding and skills are frequently called upon by the geographer, the historian, the artist, the technologist, the scientist, the games player and the musician. It is often this 'real mathematics' which is most meaningful and motivating.

School grounds present opportunities for making children aware that mathematics is 'real'. Wonder a little about the number of leaves on a tree or bricks in a wall and before you know it you'll be comparing and finding difference, adding, subtracting, multiplying and dividing. Plan to improve that space outside, perhaps by putting a few flower tubs here and there, and you'll soon be asking how much for this and that and the mathematics of economics will be staring you in the face. Make careful records of all your transactions and you will soon have more than enough data to work with.

Using the school grounds to teach mathematical skills

1. Problem solving
The mathematical problems that children are called upon to solve in the outdoor classroom are more likely to be real and relevant. They can also be discovered rather than imposed.

2. Investigation
Mathematical investigation can occur naturally and allow children to see the need for such skills as: being systematic; thinking logically; drawing inferences; drawing conclusions; presenting and justifying results.

3. Mathematical discussion
Children rarely work in isolation while they are outside. The discussion which occurs during collaboration helps to clarify their thinking because of all the explaining they have to do.

4. Algorithmic skills work provides:
- A wide variety of calculation problems.
- A need to devise procedures for solving the problems.
- Many opportunities to discover, modify and evaluate procedures.
- The chance to recognize a type of problem and solve it, confident of knowing effective methods of dealing with it.

5. Communicating mathematically
Children gain in confidence from having plenty of opportunities to apply their mathematical skills in practical situations. This helps them to see that mathematics can be a useful and precise way of communicating ideas which are important in other areas of the curriculum.

6. Choosing and using the right mathematical instruments
Mathematics outdoors is essentially practical and therefore calls for the use of measuring instruments of all kinds. Improvisation may also be needed.

7. Consolidation of learning
Learning is consolidated by meeting the same ideas in a wide variety of situations and contexts. While working outdoors, children will constantly be required to estimate, measure, calculate, collect and represent data, and to recognize shapes and patterns.

Planning for Mathematics outside

The teaching of Mathematics in primary schools usually provides two types of experiences.

1. Lessons which are clearly and mainly Mathematics. Such lessons will probably centre on an aspect of one of the National

Curriculum attainment targets and will have clearly defined learning outcomes.

2. Lessons in which Mathematics appears because of a need to use its skills or understanding to help make sense of the subject being taught. Mathematics frequently appears in Science, Technology and Geography lessons and sometimes in P.E., Art, History and Music. Sometimes this mathematics is not given any particular significance, but, at other times, it is sensible to make full use of the context provided. An example is a Science lesson where children are examining a tomato plant deprived of light for several days. They go outside to remove the covering and compare the height of the light-deprived plant with a control plant. Mathematics is used when two plants are measured and the difference in height calculated. In order to act as scientists, the children have to apply mathematical knowledge and skills centred on A.T.2 Number (comparing two numbers to find the difference) and A.T.4 Shape and Space (measuring).

Very often, opportunities for mathematical work in the school grounds come most naturally from work in other subjects. Only on rare occasions will work be started and completed in the school grounds. Normally, there is a flow between the indoor and the outdoor classroom, as shown in the example below.

PLAN OF LESSON

Concept:
Shape, regular and irregular.

Aims:
To highlight the basic terminology involved.
To recognize the difference between the two types of shape.
To see the importance of shape in simple designs, both natural and artificial.

Method:
In the classroom, a discussion centres on the terms 'regular' and 'irregular' as they apply to shape.

Outside:
The children are then challenged to explore the outdoor environment of the school, searching for examples of regular and irregular shapes.

Back inside:
Back in the classroom the children discuss their discoveries with each other and begin to form some opinions on the occurrence of regular and irregular shape in the natural and created environments in and around their school.

Safety All the activities in this book should be undertaken with commonsense safety precautions.

Litter
When carrying out activities involving litter collection, the following precautions should be taken:

Don't ask children to clear an area of litter until the caretaker has checked that none of the litter is of a type which could prove to be a health hazard, e.g. syringes.

Always ensure that the children wear gloves. You could also provide litter pickers, which can be bought for about £5.50 each.

Warn the children that some things which people throw away could make them very ill if they handled them. Such a warning will also protect them when playing in parks or on the beach.

Ponds
When children are carrying out work connected with ponds they should always be carefully supervised. This also provides opportunities to warn children about the dangers of water in general.

Number Work in the School Grounds

It is essential that children's understanding of number is developed through a very wide range of experiences. Once numerical concepts are established children need opportunities to practise and apply acquired skills. We need to demonstrate to children that numbers and the things that we do both 'to' them and 'with' them are part of our everyday lives. The outdoor classroom can provide the resources to do this.

To get to grips with number, children must do:

- Plenty of counting. Essentially, they must learn to organize and compare their counts in order to develop an understanding of place value.
- Lots of operations on numbers until they come to know all the different ways in which one number can operate on another.
- Lots of searching for pattern in number sequences so that they are continually adding to their store of experiences of the relationships which can exist between numbers.

The importance of counting

Number symbols will have more meaning when they are used to represent something the child really knows and cares about. Going outside and counting real things for real reasons motivates children far better than counting coloured plastic cubes to please the teacher.

COUNTING CHALLENGES
- Plant out ten sunflower seeds and wait to count how many germinate.
- Draw round your foot on thick transparent polythene and cut out a template. Take it outside and put it down gently on daisy-strewn grass. Count how many daisies you might have stood on. What is the highest number you might tread on? What is the lowest?

Using a polythene 'foot' template enables children to count the number of daisies they might stand on.

- How many children come through the gate in the morning with one adult? How many come with two adults? How many come on their own?
- Sit beside the biodegradable waste bin at playtime. Tally the number of children who put in each of the following: apple cores, banana skins, orange peel, pear cores, any other fruit remains. Back in the classroom record the results and publish the data.
- Choose something outside to count, of which you think that there are fewer than fifty, and see if you were right. Then count something of which you think there are more than 200, and see if you are right.
- How many bricks, to the nearest hundred, were used to build the school?
- Make lists of things outside which are best counted in ones, then go on to make a list of things which are best counted in tens and finally lists of things which are best counted in hundreds or perhaps even thousands.

All these activities will tell teachers about their children's understanding of the number system. They require children to continually restructure their existing knowledge as they use familiar ideas and procedures on new problems.

COUNTING TALK

While the 'countless' counts are going on, so too are all sorts of other things. What does the word 'countless' mean, for a start? The dictionary gives us words like 'innumerable' and 'myriad'. It can be fun making up sentences that contain these words. 'There are innumerable stars in the sky.' Could we say a 'myriad' bricks were used to build the school? What do the words 'a few' and 'a lot' mean? How many does a few mean in the sentence 'There are a few doors into the school'? Does 'few' describe the same number as in the sentence 'There are quite a few tiles on the roof'? If the question is 'Are there many snails under the stone?', how many do there have to be before the answer is 'yes'? Getting children to discuss the words we use to qualify numbers is to begin to get them fascinated with numbers themselves.

Carrying out a litter tally provides an opportunity for counting.

ORGANIZING COUNTS

Children need to understand the place value system in order to develop mathematical competency. Part of that understanding is seeing the need for the system. The children's curiosity about just how many of something there might be when there are obviously a great many can be very effectively directed towards finding a system to cope with the counting. If children can develop the understanding and competency to organize large counts and do so frequently, each experience will contribute towards a vital understanding of place value. The grounds of a school and the things which happen there provide opportunities for interesting counting activities.

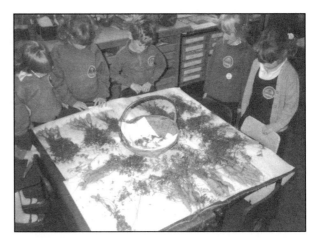

Counting carrots from the garden: putting large numbers into tens helps an understanding of place value.

- Finding a method of counting the number of seeds on a large sunflower head can be fun. The children need to discover a good way of organizing it and trial and error are a valuable part of the experience. One effective method is to use ten yogurt cartons and some margarine cartons. Very carefully count out the yogurt cartons, stressing the number ten. Put ten seeds in each carton and then tip each one into the margarine carton, counting 10 ... 20 ... 30 ... 40 ... 50 until 100 is reached. Proceed until all the seeds are counted.

- Counting the leaves lying on the ground under a tree, such as a sycamore, on a day towards the end of autumn is not beyond the ability of children who have already done a number of organized counts, though it will test their problem-solving skills. If they can carry out a complicated organizational procedure like the one described here, they will have gone a long way towards understanding the place value system.

In our example, children used lots of plastic carrier bags from the local supermarket and some of the caretaker's black plastic sacks. They organized themselves into teams of eleven, ten of whom were leaf collectors, the eleventh was the 'tallier' and team leader. Each team member collected ten leaves and queued with them. They put their leaves in the leader's plastic bag and 100 was recorded on the tally sheet. This was repeated ten times. With 1000 leaves inside it, the bag was then tied and a new one came into use. When five carrier bags were full they were put inside a black plastic sack and that was tied up and a label of 5000 attached.

- How many children can stand inside a chosen piece of playground marking at the same time? Can they come out of the marked area and arrange themselves in a way which will make them easy to count?
- Ten children in turn throw a ball against a wall and catch it ten times, each shouting out: '1 lot of 10 ... 10', '2 lots of 10 ... 20', '3 lots of 10 ... 30', until the tenth child has thrown and the magic 100 has been reached. If they repeat that whole sequence ten times then they will know that between them they have thrown and caught a ball 1000 times.

Operating on numbers

An understanding of addition, subtraction, multiplication and division and the relationships which exist between them can come through the continual requirement to think through, and solve practically in the first instance, the full range of problems which one or more of those operations could solve. When we present children with real problems which they can solve practically, even five year olds can cope with division problems!

ENCOUNTERS WITH ADDITION

Addition problems are usually arrived at either by partitioning sets into subsets or by the union of disjoint sets.

- There are seven children to help carry the P.E. baskets. Will three help with carrying the balls and the other four take the skipping ropes? (3 + 4 = 7)
- Robert has picked two apples, Ranjit five and Liz six. How many have they got altogether? (2 + 5 + 6 = 13)

ENCOUNTERS WITH SUBTRACTION

1. The need to compare two or more numbers and find the difference

   These number difference problems can be solved by counting the number of elements in two sets and then subtracting the smaller number from the larger.

How many children can fit inside the circle?

- Are there the same number of windows in the back wall of the school as there are in the side wall?
- Which are there fewer of – big or small litter bins?
- Which have we got more of – guinea pigs or rabbits?

2. The need to make two unequal groups equal

- We have planted six bulbs in the other tub but only two in this one. How many more do we need to plant to have the same number in each? (6 - 2)
- Twenty children are going to do an obstacle course. Eight have had their turn. How many more children have got to have a go before we've finished? (20 - 8)

3. The need to take away

- We planted ten tomato plants, but two failed in the dry weather. How many are left? (10 - 2)
- Thirty children want to go on the assault course but seven haven't got the right kind of shoes on. How many were allowed on? (30 - 7)

ENCOUNTERS WITH MULTIPLICATION

1. The need for repeated addition

- Six windows each have four panes of glass. How many panes are there altogether? (4 + 4 + 4 + 4 + 4 + 4 or 4 x 6)

- Some children group themselves into threes. Each group will be responsible for clearing the grounds of litter on one school day of the week. How many children have a turn in one week? (3 + 3 + 3 + 3 + 3 or 3 x 5)

2. The need for magnification

- We have six hens altogether. One hen needs 200g of grain a day, so we shall need six times that amount each day. How much is that? (200 x 6)
- There are approximately fifty bricks in each metre length of wall. The wall is five metres long. Can we work out how many bricks were used to build the wall without counting them? (50 x 5)
- How many litter bins would we have if we were to treble the number we have now?

How much grain is needed to feed six hens?

ENCOUNTERS WITH DIVISION

1. Sharing problems (partition)

- We need to get into equal groups to play some ring games. There are twenty-eight children. Let's suppose we got into four groups. How many would there be in each group? (28 ÷ 4)
- The hen coop is 18 decimetres long. If we wanted to section it into three equal spaces, how long would each section be? (18 ÷ 3)

2. Grouping problems (quotition)

- Thirty children are going to carry out a mini-beast hunt in the grounds. If they work in groups of three, how many groups will there be? (30 ÷ 3)
- We spend £5 a week on animal food for the hens and the rabbits. Will £60 be enough for a ten week term? (60 ÷ 10)

Learning new concepts

Up to this point examples of work, though not the principles, have been appropriate for children in reception and years 1 to 3. As children progress through the different levels of the National Curriculum the counting and calculation problems offered to them should involve the use of higher numbers. When a new property of numbers has been met in the classroom – odd and even, multiple, prime, triangular, square, etc. – or a new aspect of number, such as fractions or ratio, has been explored, it is not difficult to explore it further outside. The tables of activities for Key Stages 1 and 2 (on pp.14–19) give numerous examples of how to involve children in increasingly challenging activities which require them to apply and therefore deepen their understanding of newly acquired concepts. A few examples are singled out here to provide an introduction to those tables.

ENCOUNTERS WITH SOME SPECIAL PROPERTIES AND CONCEPTS OF NUMBER

- If we want to plant out the flower tubs with tulips so that the colours are alternately red and yellow, should we plant an odd or an even number of bulbs?
- There are twenty-five children here today and we want two equal teams. Is that number going to make it easy or awkward?
- Plan a prime number flower bed.
- **Red number days**   Make use of number snakes or 100 squares marked out on the playground. Outline with red chalk:
    Square numbers on Monday.
    Prime numbers on Tuesday.
    Factors of 100 on Wednesday.
    Multiples of 4 on Thursday.
    Triangular numbers on Friday.

A number snake in the playground can be used for a variety of number activities.

Each day the children have to fathom out the reason for the red outlines which have been put round the numbers by their teacher. Solutions written on a slip of paper are posted in a box. At the end of the day the solutions can be compared and discussed.

- **Ratios** Work out ratios of children to balls, skipping ropes, any other piece of small games equipment; ratio of children to benches in the playground; ratio of children to bulbs that need planting, sets of forks and trowels, flower tubs.

Working out the ratio of children to games equipment.

- **Fractions** When activities are planned outside try giving the instructions in fractional terms: 1/10 of the class will hunt mini-beasts, 1/3 will do weather recordings, 1/5 will pond dip. How many children are left to do the evaporation experiment?

Look out for opportunities to ask questions such as:
- Do more or less than 1/3 of the children enter school by the side gate?
- Could 1/4 of the class sit on the bench at the same time?
- What fraction of the 100 bulbs we planted has survived the slugs?
- What percentage of the school grounds is laid down to grass?

ALGEBRA ALONGSIDE THE NUMBER

Continual exploration of number patterns and relationships is the foundation that needs to be laid as a sound basis for algebra. If every time children handle numbers they are encouraged to be enthusiastic pattern spotters that in its turn will help them in the search for relationships which lies at the heart of mathematics. Activities which lead to generalization and encourage children to substitute symbols for words promote algebraic understanding. With these principles in mind, some of the tabled activities have an algebra heading. The examples do not extend beyond National Curriculum Level 4 work, since sound teaching in this area will result in children being able to work in symbolic form by this stage.

A game of marbles helps the children practise using numbers.

Developing an understanding of our number system through the outdoor classroom   Key Stage 1
(all use of standard metric units involves use of place value)

	Pond	Animals	Pathways and Visitors	Allotment, Trees and Shrubs	Buildings	Conservation Area	Games and Activities	Weather
Counting 10 100 1000	How many tadpoles, pond-skaters, snails, and lilypads are there?	Counting animals and offspring. Can you count the grains in a handful?	Count the number of stones in a pathway.	Counts of crops: radishes in row, leaves on stems, petals on flowers, fruit in box.	Count bricks or stones in a row along the side of a building.	Counts within a quadrant or a specific area – mini-beasts, grasses, flowers.	Counting children in activities. 'Get into groups of ?' Counting equipment.	Counting for measurement – cm or ml of rainfall.
Organizing Counts: 2s, 5s, 10s, etc.	Can you think of a way of checking how many tadpoles there are?	Tallying collections of eggs, packing them into boxes of 6. Organize counts into 10s.	Tally the people using a particular pathway. Is there a pattern in their use?	Find a way to organize these counts.	How many bricks in a wall?	A tally or count of birds using the area.	Organizing the count.	Counting/tallying days of sun, rain, etc. on a weather chart.
Number line	There are 10 lilypads across the pond, a frog is on the second one. How many more to cross?	There are 20 chickens on a perch, you have fed the first 3. How many more to be fed?	There are 15 stones, you are on the 6th. How many more to the end?	There is a row of 20 plants and we weed out every other one. How many are left?	The wall is 100 bricks long. We have laid 57, how many more must we lay?	There are 10 leaves along a branch. The caterpillar has eaten the first 7. How many more has he got to eat?	30 children are waiting to try throwing. The first 10 have had a go. How many before you if you are no. 28?	We are keeping a weather chart for each day in a number line. What was the 9th day, 15th day, 21st day?
Fractions	Can you fold a lilypad in half? Can you quarter it?	We have collected 12 eggs and we sell half. The hens should let the grass grow in half their run.	If Jo is standing halfway along a 25m path, where is she?	Cut an apple in $\frac{1}{2}$, $\frac{1}{4}$. We have 250g of beans and we give away half. How much do we have left?	How many bricks would you need if the wall was half as long?	If your quadrant is half as big, do you see half the numbers of species?	'I think your circle should be half as big.'	A quarter of September was rainy – how many days was that?
Estimates	Estimate how many tadpoles in 1 scoop. Round off to the nearest 10 or 100. Estimate how many in the whole pond.	Estimate how many eggs you will collect in a week.	How far do you think it is along the paths?	Any of these counts should be estimated first, either into weight or quantity and rounded off if wanted.	Estimate before all the above calculations and counts.	Estimate before counts. Using information, estimate how many there are in whole area.	Estimates of throwing, jumping distances.	Estimate rainfall, hours of sunshine, sunny days, times of day.

Developing an understanding of our number system through the outdoor classroom — Key Stage 2

	Pond	Animals	Pathways and visitors	Allotment, Trees and Shrubs	Buildings	Conservation Area	Games and Activities	Weather
Organizing counting and understanding relationships X 10 X 100 **Averages**	Take 2 samples from pond. Count tadpoles. Compare counts. How many if there were 10 samples? or 100 samples?	Work out the food needed by weight for 1 day, 2 days, 3 days. How much for 10 days or even 100?	Compare lengths of paths using both m and cm. How long would our path be if it was 10 times as long? What is the average number of visitors in a week?	Recording crops by quantity or weight, expressing as kg or g. 1 plant produces 253 g of fruit. What do 10 plants produce? Average yields.	Measuring windows and doors in buildings (m or cm). Area of glass. How much glass for 10 windows? 100 windows?	Counting samples of mini-beasts and flora. If ? in 1 area how many in 10 areas are the same? What is the average number of snails/spiders, etc.?	Measuring time in games involves understanding higher numbers. If you can run X m in 1 min. how far in 10 min. or 60 min.? What is the average number of catches in 1 min.?	Keeping a record of rainfall over a time. Keep a record of hours of sunshine in a week. Find average.
Fractions	How many if the sample is half as many?	We have 12 rabbits. If we give 2 away, what fraction less food will we need for a week?		If we grow 3 kg 500 g of potatoes, for 8 classes, each should have 1/8 of crop.				Measure rainfall in litres and millilitres.
Decimals	Measure the perimeter and express in m and cm.		Measure shortest and longest routes. Express in m and cm.					
Percentages	Measure area and work out percentage covered by lily-pads.	What percentage of their body weight do the animals eat?	What percentage of visitors come in through main gate? Which are most popular paths?	Weigh beans, prepare to eat and work out percentage of waste.	Work out area of a wall and then percentage of area not brick.	What percentage of mini-beasts are snails, ants, woodlice, etc.?	The children like different games. Count the total and find percentage for each game.	Calculate the percentage of time in a day that was sunny.
Ratio		Can you express it as a ratio?			Is the ratio of door to height of wall always the same?	Observe numbers of 2 bird species over a week. Work out ratio between the two. Draw a plan to scale.		Calculate a ratio of sun: cloud time. Height/shadow ratios.
Scale	Draw a plan of the pond to scale.	Draw a plan of animal homes to scale.	Draw a plan to scale of our routeways.	Draw a plan to scale of allotment.	Draw a plan of building to scale.			
Negative numbers	Measure the temperature in winter. How cold does it get?	What happens if the temperature is below zero?						Measuring temperature when below freezing.
Estimates and refining methods	Estimate total weight of frog spawn. Devise a way of finding out.	Estimate weights and cost of feed.	Estimate distances and times around school.	Estimate yields. Count 1 plant and refine estimate.	Estimate bricks in a wall. Count 1 row. How many rows?	Estimate and refine all these counts.	Estimate and refine any counts.	Estimate today's temperature. Look at records. Refine ideas.

Problems to solve, using mathematical operations, provoked by the outdoor classroom — Key Stage 1

	Pond	Animals	Pathways and Visitors	Allotment, Trees and Shrubs	Buildings	Conservation Area	Games and Activities	Weather
Addition — Union of disjoint sets	When pond dipping, John had 4 tadpoles, Idi had 6. (4 + 6)	3 rabbits sleep in 1 hutch, 6 in the other. (3 + 6)	It is 20 m to the pets and 10 m further to the pond. (20 m + 10 m = 30 m)	16 beans on this plant and 12 on that one. (16 + 12)	There are 8 windows at the front and 6 at the back. (8 + 6)	Ann saw 7 red, 4 blue flowers. (7 + 4)	8 children on the frame, 8 more came on. (8 + 8)	Sun for 2 hours a.m., 3 hours p.m. (2 + 3 = 5 hours)
Addition — Partition of sets	£10 spent on water plants: £6 on lilies and £4 on iris. (£6 + £4)	6 bantams: 3 in the coop and 3 outside. (6 = 3 + 3)	8 visitors: 4 parents, the milkman and 3 men to cut grass. (8 = 4 + 1 + 3)	20 potatoes from 1 plant: 12 for prints, 8 for cooking. (20 = 12 + 8)	30 children in the class, 21 inside and 9 outside. (30 = 21 + 9)	We sorted 12 flowers by colour. 3 pink, 4 blue, 5 yellow. (12 = 4 + 5 + 3)	There were 15 children: 6 playing catch, 4 playing ball, 5 talking. (15 = 6 + 4 + 5)	Our chart for 7 days: 2 sunny, 3 cloudy, 2 wet. (7 = 2 + 3 + 2)
Subtraction — Take away	We had £5, and spent £2 on plants. (£5 – £2)	The big hens need 12 scoops of corn and the small ones need 4.	We expected 12 visitors but 4 couldn't come. (12 – 4 = 6)	We hung up 8 bird feeders, but 2 fell off. (8 – 2 = 6)	The wall was high; we took 2 rows off. (12 – 2 = 10 rows)	There were 6 birds on a branch and 4 flew away. (6 – 4 = 2 left)	'Sue has 10 in her team and I only have 8.' (10 – 8 = 2)	Temperature was 20° this morning, but it has fallen 2°. (20° – 2° = 18°)
Subtraction — Difference	12 children by the pond, 7 see frogs, 5 don't. 12 – 7 = 5	The difference is 12 – 4 = 6	This path is 30 m, that one is 20 m. (30 m – 20 m)	We got 36 apples from this tree and 24 from that one (36 – 24).	This door is 210 cm high, that is 200 cm. The difference is 210 – 200 = 10 cm.	9 flowers and 5 grasses. (9 – 5 = 4 difference)	I can throw a ball up 180 cm, but the netball hoop is 300 cm. (300 – 180 = 120 cm more)	The temperature today is 19°. Yesterday it was 23°. (23° – 19° = 4°)
Subtraction — Inverse addition	Find 9 creatures. 4 found. How many more?	We need £12 to buy a rabbit. We have £10. (£12 – £10 = £2)	We need 30 stones to lay a path and we only have 22. We need 30 – 22 = 8.	We had £1 for seeds. We spent 65p. We have 100p – 65 = 35 left.	9 hours to paint the wall. 6 hours done. (9 – 6 = 3 more)	We want 10 ants; we have 5. (10 – 5 = 5 more)		
Multiplication — Repeated addition	8 tadpoles, each have 2 legs. (2 + 2 + 2 + 2 + 2 + 2 or 2 x 8)	It takes 10 min. to clean a rabbit cage and we have 3 to clean. £2 a week to feed the hens.	3 gardeners came to school. Each planted 3 trees. (3 x 3 = 9)	5 lettuces in each row, 3 rows. (5 x 3, or 5 + 5 + 5).	There are 12 windows each with 4 panes (4 x 12).	6 children each planted 3 bulbs. (6 x 3)	We need 10 new balls and they cost 35p each.	
Multiplication — Magnification	A pond snail is 7mm. Find one twice as big.	For twice as many?	This path is 25 m. We want one 3 times as long.	This Christmas tree is 50 cm tall. That one is 3 times as tall. (50 cm x 3)	The hall is 3 times taller than the classrooms (5 m x 4)	Count the petals of a buttercup. 3 times as many = 5 x 3	There are 12 children in our circle, but we want one 3 times as big.	There were 4 cm of rain last week and 3 times as much this week. (4 x 3 = 12 cm)
Division — Partition	An hour to top up the pond: 5 children take fair turns. How long must each work?	Share 6 carrots between 2 rabbits. (6 ÷ 2 = 3)	5 children showed round 15 visitors. (15 ÷ 5 = 3 each)	If we plant 26 tomato plants in 2 rows, how many in each? (26 ÷ 2)	A room has 4 walls and 8 windows. How could they be put in fairly? (8 ÷ 4 = 2)	4 children will collect litter for 20 days. (20 ÷ 4 = 5 days each)	There were 10 children and 5 slides. (10 ÷ 5 = 2 on each)	There are 60 min. in 1 hour. Make a timer for sun/shade and mark it every 15 min. How many marks for 1 hr?
Division — Quotition	15 plants in groups of 3. (15 ÷ 3 = 5 groups).	Hutches are 50 cm long. How many will fit into 3m? (300 ÷ 50 = 6)	16 children walked along the path in twos (16 ÷ 2 = 8 pairs).	We have 20 bulbs to plant and want 4 in a row. (20 ÷ 4 = 5 rows)	A brick is 20 cm. If we lay a metre row, 100 ÷ 20 cm = 5 bricks.	3 can sit in the bird hide. If our class is 30, how many groups? (30÷3)	32 children got into groups of 4. (32 ÷ 4 = 8 groups)	

Problems to solve, using mathematical operations, provoked by the outdoor classroom   Key Stage 2

	Pond	Animals	Pathways and Visitors	Allotment, Trees and Shrubs	Buildings	Conservation Area	Games and Activities	Weather
Addition Union of disjoint sets / Partition of sets	One sample of frogspawn is 236 g, the other 349 g. Total? The perimeter is 4.35 m, 1.22 m paved and 3.13 m grassed.	The rabbits cost £2.65 to feed a week, the hens £2.17. Total? We use 695 g of feed a day. 390 g rabbits + 305 g hens.	The edging to our paths is 362 cm + 439 cm. 126 cars go past in 10 min. 52 red + 26 blue + 23 white + 12 green + 13 metallic.	2 packets of seeds (96 + 87) We had 437 seedlings: 120 peas, 94 tomatoes, 123 beans.	The length of the classroom is 12 m 32 cm and the width is 10 m 57 cm. The perimeter = (12.32 x 2) + (10.57 x 2)	We find 52 ants in 1 quadrant and 173 in another. (152 + 173) 137 birds visited our table: sparrows 56 times and others 81 times.	Keeping a record of scores for games, especially those with dart type scoring.	216 ml rain fell on Mon. and 79 ml fell on Tues. (216 + 79 = ?) The rainfall for the week was: 0 + 72 + 112 + 237 + 0
Subtraction Take away / Difference / Inverse addition	Use 2 buckets to fill our pond. One holds ? The other holds ? What is the difference or how much more to be the same?	Our food fund for animals was £10. We spent £5.60. How much left? (£10 – £5.60) The big hens have laid 62 eggs and the bantams 43. The difference is: 62 – 43 or ?	One path is 10 m 32 cm long and the other is 12 m 15 cm. What is the difference? (12.15 – 10.32 m 1215 – 1032 cm) How much more to be the same?	One packet of seeds had 115 in and the other only had 76. What is the difference? (115 – 76) How many more would we need to have the same?	It costs £56 to hire our hall for an afternoon, or £20 an hour. Which is cheaper and by how much? (£20 x 3) – £56.	We watch in the hide for 75 min. each day but today for 18 min. less (75 – 18) Sample shows 350 woodlice in one habitat and 215 in another. (350 – 215)	Tim can kick a ball 10 m 64 cm, Amy can kick one 12 m 36 cm. What is the difference (1236 – 1064) or how much further will Tim have to kick to equal Amy?	There were 5 hr 36 min. of sunshine on Tues. and 3 hr 47 min. on Wed. What was the difference? (5 hr 36 min. – 3 hr 47 min)
Multiplication Repeated addition / Magnification	If there are 25 tadpoles in 1 sample, how many in 15? Estimate how many in a sample 10 times as big as the first.	Each cage needs 67 cm of wire. We have 15 cages. This rabbit has grown so much it needs 3 times as much food. (50 g x 3 = 150 g)	The milkman always leaves 12 pints. How many are left in June? The gardener charges £2.30 an hour. She works 15 hours.	28 potatoes under one plant, 18 plants. Estimate total. (28 x 18) A courgette is 27 cm long, but a marrow is $2\frac{1}{2}$ times as long.	The length of the classroom is 16 m 27 cm and the width is 10 m 12 cm. The area is 1627 x 1012.	We feed birds 150 g of seed a day. In a month? I think a maple leaf is 12 times bigger than an apple leaf of 32 cm². (32 x 12)	We can run round the field in 49 seconds. How long do you think it will take to do it 18 times?	
Division Partition / Quotition	We want to pave round our pond. The perimeter is 4 m 30 cm, each paving stone is 40 cm across. How many can we use?	69 days this term to feed the hens, our class is 28. How many goes can we have? Rota: 102 possible hours in 4 weeks, 30 children.	We have 2 hours to show people round the school. How long each for 15 people? For a path of 554 cm how many stones of 30 cm?	The row is 372 cm long and we have 24 plants. How much space each? (372 ÷ 24) If each needs 30 cm how many could we plant?	A brick is 14 cm, the wall is 16 m 20 cm. How many bricks in each row? If we use 84 bricks, how long is each?	6 hrs 15 min. in a day and 32 in our class, so we can watch the bird table in ones (6 h 15 min ÷ 32) or in pairs (6 h 15 min ÷ (32 ÷ 2))	We have £9.75. If each ball costs 89p, how many can we buy? We have £9.75 and we need 10 balls. What can we pay for each?	The sun moves through 1 section of our sundial in 18 min. How many sections will it move through from 9 o'clock to 3.15?

Developing an understanding of algebra through the outdoor classroom   Key Stage 1

	Pond	Animals	Pathways and Visitors	Allotment, Trees and Shrubs	Buildings	Conservation Area	Games and Activities	Weather
Patterns	The first lilypad has 1 frog, the second has 2 ... continue the pattern.	Our eggs are arranged: 2 large, 1 bantam, 2 large, etc.	We made our path using a pattern of oblong and hexagonal slabs.	We planted our rows in a pattern: 2 short crops, 1 tall crop ...	Look for patterns in bricks in walls.	Design a border for your chart, with a pattern of flowers or mini-beasts.	We ran round in a pattern – running/hopping.	Design a pattern of weather symbols for your recording sheet.
Patterns in addition and subtraction	10 frogs on a lilypad. 1 at a time jumps into the water: $10 - 1 = 9$, etc.	Find all the ways 10 eggs can be shared between 2 people. $9 + 1$, etc.	There are 2 children to guide 5 visitors. How could they organize it?	There are 10 apples and 2 people ... $10 + 0$, $9 + 1$, etc.	Make a staircase with bricks. $0 + 1 = 1$ $1 + 1 = 2 ...$	We pick 8 grasses and share them out: $8 + 0$ $8 - 1$ $7 + 1$ or $7 - 2$	Show a pattern in the ways teams could be made. Which way is fair?	How many sunny/cloudy days could we have had in 10 days? $10 + 0$, $9 + 1$, etc.
Odds and Evens	When is there an even number of frogs on the lilypad?	Which ways will give both an even number of eggs?	Count pupils on the path in pairs. Which numbers do you miss?	We have planted our onions in even numbers.	Count the bricks in a row. Are they odd or even?	Count the legs on mini-beasts. Do any have an odd number?	We play this game in pairs. There are 15 – can we do it?	Count the rainy days this month. Is it an odd or even number?
Using a symbol	I know we have 8 fish. I can only see 3. $? + 3 = 8$ $8 - 3 = ?$	We have 12 rabbits, 7 are in the sun, so ? must be inside.	We expect 15 visitors today. 5 have arrived. ? to come.	We planted 10 potatoes and pulled up 5 plants. $10 - 5 = ?$	There are 20 windows. 18 cleaned. $? + 18 = 20$ left to do.	We saw 18 birds, 14 were sparrows and ? were blackbirds.	16 children, 12 on the frame. $12 + ? = 16$ How many on the slide?	There are 30 days in June. If 25 were cloudy, how many were sunny? $30 - 25 = ?$
Patterns in 2s, 5s, 10s, etc. **Strategies with 10**	The bulrushes grow in clumps of 2s, 5s, 10s, etc.	Eggs are packed in boxes of 6. There are 26 chicks. $(10 + 10 + 6)$	5 pupils at a time can go along the path. How many have gone? Can they fit into 5s?	We sell our carrots for 10p a bag. There are 13 apples in the box. We pick them in 10s. $13 + 10$, $23 + 10$	The wall is 9 rows high, 10 bricks per row. How many bricks are used after each row?	We saw 32 ants and 25 woodlice. $30 + 2 + 20 + 5$. $50 + 7$. 57 altogether.	We brought our bikes to school – 2 wheels. Our scooters – 3 wheels. Our roller skates – 4 wheels.	
Function Machines	The magic fish pond changes every tadpole, fish or plant by size or shape or number.	Every time rabbits go down the burrow 3 times as many come out. $(4 \times 3 = 12)$	How ever many people go along this path, double the number come back.	We have 24 bean plants. Next year we will have half as many.		This leaf changes any creatures who land on it by a mathematical rule $(+2 \times 4)$	When we play marbles each time I win a point I get + 3 of your marbles.	Every time a ray of sun/drop of rain lands on this plant it increases its yield $\times 2$.

Developing an understanding of algebra through the outdoor classroom   Key Stage 2

	Pond	Animals	Pathways and Visitors	Allotment, Trees and Shrubs	Buildings	Conservation Area	Games and Activities	Weather
Generalizing Patterns to include multiples, factors, squares	Draw a plan to scale – find out the area. What will be the area if you double it or halve it?	A large egg tray has 12 rows of 12. 12 x 12 = 144. Find all the arrangements that can be expressed as 2 factors and explain them.	Our pathway is 35 m long. We want to edge both sides with strips of wood 3 m long. Work out a table to show the multiples of 3, that will show the position of each strip. x | 1 2 3 4 3 | 3 6 9 12 etc.	Each carrot seed grows carrots that are multiplied by 3 and have 6 added: Seeds Carrots 2 x3 +6 12 3 x3 +6 15 4 x3 +6 ?	Draw up a table to show the bricks needed to build a wall 10 rows high with 8, 9, 10, 11, 12 in each row. x | 1 2 3 4... 8 | 8 16 24 32... 9 | 9 18 27 36... 10 | 10 20 30 40... Explain what happens.	We use 4 equal pieces of wood to make a quadrant. How many of the same pieces do we need to make one twice as big, 3 times as big? Show it in a diagram. What pattern can you see in the totals each time?	Draw a mini tennis court on the playground. Make one double the size. What happens to the edges and the area? Is there enough space to double it again? Using tallying in games scoring to help understand place value.	
Using double and halving	Start with an even number of tadpoles. Work out what happens if this number keeps doubling. Now try starting with an odd number.							
Inverse operations		÷ | 144 144 144 2 | 72 3 | 48 4 | 36 etc.		Tallying in keeping records of crops helps with place value.				
Function machines								
Using simple formulae in words	If I halve the number of tadpoles and – 7 and the answer is 8, how many did I have?	If I double the weight of rabbit food and + 60 g, I have 460 g. What did I start with?	If I walk round the school 3 times quicker and it takes me 39 min 30 sec, what used I to do it in?	If I put the tomatoes in 6 equal rows of 8 + 2, how many are there?	There are 32 windows in our school, each wall has 4. How many walls are there?	Our records of birds show that on Tuesday we saw half the number of birds + 2 than Monday, which was 22. ? + 2 = 22 ÷ 2	If you score 1 goal it = 5. If you score 5 goals you + 5 extra. What will you score for 6 goals?	There were twice as many hours of sunshine in week 2, than week 1. Week 2 = 33. Week 1 = 33 ÷ 2
Co-ordinates	Draw a scale plan. Draw the pond using turtle graphics. Draw a graph to show changes in temperature over time.	Plot the rabbit hutches on a plan of the enclosure. Use a graph to record egg collection over a month.	Use a graph to record the fluctuations of use of a path during the day.	Plot the trees on a plan of the grounds. Plot the planting scheme on a plan of the allotment using co-ordinates.	Draw shapes using turtle graphics to represent accurately our school buildings.	Draw a graph to show the number of a species in each habitat.	Where do play activities take place in the playground? Plot their positions on a plan using co-ordinates.	Draw a graph to show fluctuation in rainfall over time, or sunshine times.

Beyond this level algebra has become very abstract and does not seem appropriate in this form.

Cutting apples into halves and quarters provides a tangible way of looking at fractions.

How long does it take for the sun to move through one section of the sundial?

Windows Challenge

Get ready to go outside. You will need to take a pencil, some paper and a clipboard. Walk right round the school building and every time you see a window draw a small rectangle on your paper. Inside the rectangle write down the number of panes of glass in the window.

Back in the classroom

Answer these questions.
You will need to count and calculate.

1. How many windows does the school have in its outside walls?
2. How many of the windows have more than one pane of glass?
3. If the number of windows in the school was doubled, how many would there be?
4. How many of the windows in the school have an odd number of panes of glass in them?

A Litter Collection Challenge

You are going outside. Before you go make a list of the names of all the children in the group. Each of you should take a plastic carrier bag and you should protect yourself from germs by wearing gloves because you are going to pick up litter!

Working individually, pick up as many pieces of litter as you can in 10 minutes. At the end of that time count the pieces of litter you have collected as you put them in the dustbin.

Back in the classroom

Beside your name on the list enter the number of pieces of litter you have picked up.

Now answer these questions.

1. What was the total number of pieces of litter picked up by the group?
2. What was the highest number of pieces of litter that anybody collected?
3. What was the lowest number of pieces of litter that anybody picked up?
4. What was the number difference between the highest and the lowest scores?

Make a new list of names and the number of pieces of litter collected. Start with the lowest number and finish with the highest.

PHOTOCOPIABLE

Natural Numbers Challenge

Look at this number pattern. It is called the Fibonacci sequence.

0+1	1+2	2+3	3+5	5+8	8+13	13+21	21+34	34+55
1	3	5	8	13	21	34	55	89

Find out all you can about the mathematician who discovered the pattern.

Some of the most beautiful shapes in nature contain numbers that are in the Fibonacci sequence. They are waiting for you to discover them!

Find a pine cone. Look careful-ly at the arrangement of the spirals. One set of spirals is in a clockwise direction and the other is anti-clockwise. Count each set. You should be able to find five and eight, numbers which are in the Fibonacci sequence.

Take a magnifying glass and go outside into the school grounds.

Find a daisy and look at the centre of it. It is composed of tiny florets. You will find that, like the pine cone, the florets are arranged in opposite sets of spirals. Count the spirals and see what you find.

Now look at the leaves of plants. Can you see any patterns in the way they grow round the stems? If you look hard enough you will find more Fibonacci numbers.

It is an exciting moment when you first find out how much numbers are a part of the natural world. Happy hunting!

PHOTOCOPIABLE

Measurement in the School Grounds

The measuring skills of adults are remarkably complex. Every day of our lives we are called upon to apply our knowledge of measurement routinely in a wide variety of situations.

For children, measuring can provide important mathematical experiences in relation to bases and place value, number operations and spatial understanding. Investigations in the school grounds enable children to encounter problems that call for the need to measure in a situation that makes sense to them. Children can be taught about measurement in such a way that they realize its importance as a life skill and gain sufficient practice to become both competent and confident when responding to a wide range of measurement problems.

Measuring the girth of a tree-trunk

When children are measuring using the metric system they are getting valuable experience of working in base 10. When using the imperial system or measuring time they are gaining knowledge of other bases. The experience of constantly changing units can make a significant contribution to real understanding of place value, provided that we make children aware of the processes they are using.

Children who are measuring quantify their measurements by using numbers. As they compare one measurement with another they are constantly being called upon to operate on those numbers by the use of addition, subtraction, multiplication and division. If David wants to know how much taller his sunflower is than Rachael's, subtraction will provide the answer to this 'find the difference' problem. If Rachael wants to know how much catching up her plant has to do, subtraction will provide the answer to her 'inverse addition' problem too. If children have different problems to solve and discover that the same operation will solve both of them, all-important connections may be made. Measuring also facilitates the development of spatial understanding as children explore shape, size, space inside and space taken up.

Children need to choose appropriate measuring equipment for each task.

ENCOUNTERS WITH MEASUREMENT

1. Using standard and non-standard units

- How many jumps can you do while your friend runs round the playground?
- How many skipping ropes long is the path?
- Measure the hopscotch rectangle in metres.
- Find out how many minutes and seconds it takes you to throw a ball against the wall and catch it thirty times.

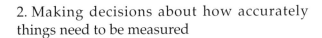

Children can use skipping ropes to measure features in the school grounds.

Planting flower tubs provides plenty of opportunities for measuring and making comparisons.

2. Making decisions about how accurately things need to be measured

- Potting compost is expensive. How much do we need to buy to fill the flower tubs?
- In the 'tallest sunflower' competition, the two tallest flowers appear to be very nearly the same height. What units are needed to measure them?

3. Choosing appropriate measuring equipment

What equipment do you need:
- To measure the height of the bench?
- To measure the air temperature under the verandah?
- To find out how much water the bird bath holds?

4. Making sensible estimates of measurements

- Estimate how many children can sit in the shade of the apple tree at the same time.
- Estimate how many times you can fill the watering can from the water butt.
- Estimate how long it will take to weed the flower bed.

How many times can the watering can be filled from the water butt?

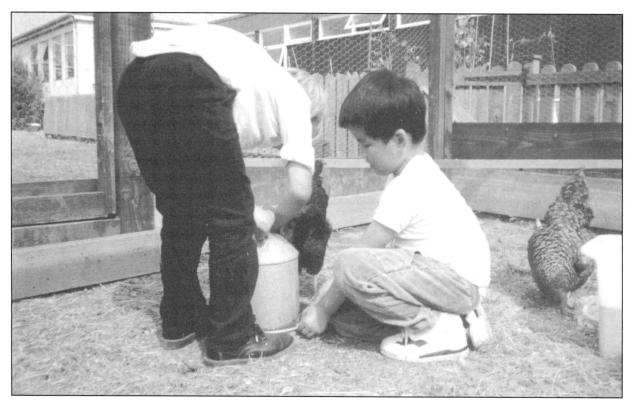

Animal feed has to be measured and costs worked out.

The weight of school animals can
be monitored at regular intervals.

Measurement in the outdoor classroom   Key Stage 1
(Moving from comparative language to standard units. Where appropriate, estimate first.)

	Pond	Animals	Pathways and Visitors	Allotment, Trees and Shrubs	Buildings	Conservation Area	Games and Activities	Weather
Size length height width	Opportunities for qualifying language. Which is biggest lilypad? How far can a frog jump?	Comparisons of length and height. Growth over a year. Length and height of hutches and enclosure.	Length and width of paths. Which is the shortest route to the front door?	Comparison of length of stems, etc. measured as growth over time. Length of rows, spaces between plants.	Length of buildings. Distances between buildings. Can we measure the height? Length/height of doors/windows.	Comparison of plants, mini-beasts. Are there seasonal changes in size?	Length and width of games courts. How high can a ball bounce?	Measure length of shadows (at different times of day).
Weight mass	What is the heaviest frog that can sit on a lilypad?	Growth in weight over a year. Weight of daily food, how much in a week? Weight of bedding.	Find out weight of post bag. Compare shovels of gravel and bark: which is heavier?	Weight of harvested produce. How many in a kilo? How heavy is a bag of compost?	Weight of bricks and stones.	Describe leaves, grasses, insects in terms of weight. Could you weigh them?	Compare weight of various balls. Does it affect what the ball does?	Does a wind sock need to be heavy or light? Choose a good material.
Volume and capacity	Topping up the pond. How many buckets will it take?	Water that each animal needs in a day. Best size of water bowl. Appropriate size of hutch for each.	How much bark fills a sack to lay on our pathway? How many sacks do we need?	How much water do plants need? How much water is in a can?	How many people fit comfortably into different parts of the building?	How much bird food fills the feeders? How many people fit into the hide?	How much water do we need to fill the water tray? How much sand to fill the sandpit?	How much rain fell yesterday? How much fell last week?
Money cost	Economics of pond management. How much are fish? Choose weeds that will total £1.00.	How much do pets cost to buy and to feed? Economics of selling our eggs.	Compare costs of slabs, sacks of gravel or bark. Which shall we lay a path with?	How much do seeds and plants cost? How much can we sell produce for?	Does this building make any money?	How much does bird seed cost? Can we buy wild flower seeds? Are seeds ever free?	What do new balls cost? How much per lap will our sponsored run make?	
Time	Changes by month and season. How long does it have to rain to raise the level? Life cycles.	Rota for care. Seasonal changes. Time each task takes.	How long does it take you to run, hop, skip round our paths?	Cycles from planting to harvest. Rotas for watering and weeding.	How long does it take to show someone round the school? Which parts are used most?	Seasonal changes. Life cycles. Rota for use of hide.	Time taken to walk/run round the field. Time taken to climb over the apparatus.	Keep a record of weather. How long did the rain last? How long was it sunny today? Where is the sun a.m./p.m.?

Measurement in the outdoor classroom   Key Stage 2

	Pond	Animals	Pathways and Visitors	Allotment, Trees and Shrubs	Buildings	Conservation Area	Games and Activities	Weather
Size length height width	Find out perimeter and area of pond. Design a pond with the same perimeter. Need it have the same area?	Are all rabbits the same height/length/girth? Record the range. What is the average?	Length of edging needed for pathways. Draw a map of paths showing distances.	Weigh bean pods – find average. Find height of trees (clinometer), girth of trunks. Area of shade.	Calculate area of floor space. Measure perimeter. Draw a plan to scale.	Are all snails, etc. the same length? What is the range? Investigate life within a quadrant.	Plan an investigation to find out the average distance your class can jump/throw.	Measure length of shadows at different times of day. Compare them.
Weight mass	How much does a tadpole weigh? Which units will you use? How can you weigh it without killing it?	Compare weights of animals with what they eat. Is there a ratio of animal: feed?	How heavy do you think a stone is? How would you weigh it? What units?	More accurate survey of weight of crops. Percentage of total in each plant.	Compare weights of building materials. How much would a barrow of each weigh?	Record how much food the wild birds eat. Try to decide which birds eat the most.	Who can jump highest? Does weight of person affect it? Ratio of weight to height.	What sort of materials would be best to measure wind strength? What is the maximum weight you could use?
Volume and Capacity	Measure the water needed to fill the fish tank. Estimate how much water is in the pond.	Make a calibrated bottle for water. Keep a record of how much water the animals drink.	Compare various path coverings. How much of each would we need for a path?	Record water for plants. Are some thirstier? Prove your answer by records.	How much does the rain butt hold? How much water in a length of drain pipe?	How much water will we need in the bird bath? How much do the birds drink?	Work out how much water is in a beaker. How much will we need for the whole class?	Keep records of rainfall for 3 months. Compare them.
Money cost	Make a shopping list of fish and plants for our pond. How much will it cost?	Economics of keeping animals. How much do all items cost? What is offset by selling young/eggs?	Which visitors pay to come to school. Why? Can we sell anything?	Use a catalogue to cost out seeds. What profit can we make by selling seedlings or produce?	What does this building cost to run? Plan an improvement and find out the cost.	Choose 5 trees you would like to buy. Find out how much they would cost. Can we afford it?	We have £100 for new play equipment. Make a shopping list, with reasons.	
Time	Draw up a timetable showing the activities of pond life.	How long do animals sleep/eat? Do hens always lay eggs at same time?	Compare routes around the school. Time quickest/slowest. Average time to look round.	Keep a record of growth. Make a timetable of duties. How long to dig, weed, water?	How long does it take to clean the building? How could you help? Timetable for use of building.	Watch a minibeast over a time. Record its movement as a percentage of the time.	Can everyone walk/run/hop/bike around the school in the same time? Timetable for use of field, etc.	Make a sundial.

A playground with painted shapes and numbers provides unlimited opportunities for mathematical activities.

When the vegetables have been harvested they can be counted, sorted and weighed.

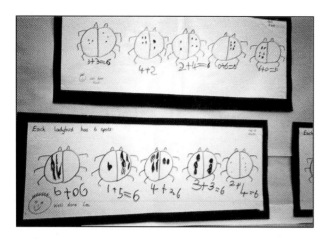

Observations of wildlife in the school grounds can be used as a basis for number work.

The apple harvest is sorted into groups of ten.

In autumn, leaf counts can be organized: the large numbers encountered will help develop an understanding of place value.

Children take a special interest in measuring the growth of their own plants.

Measuring play equipment provides practice in using tape measures.

Observing and drawing the shapes around them gives children an introduction to geometry.

Collecting and recording data by the school pond.

The results of a survey on taste form an introduction to data handling for young learners.

Shadow lengths can be compared at different times of day.

A rain gauge in the school grounds will enable records of rainfall to be kept over a specific period.

Tree Challenge

Choose a tree in the school grounds. Use a clinometer to find out its height.

Imagine that the tree is diseased and must be cut down. You have been given the job of finding out which way it should fall if it is to do the least damage.

Starting from the trunk, mark out the tree's length along the ground as far as possible, in four directions: North, South, East and West.

Make a table like this and list all the things the tree would fall on in each direction.

North	South	East	West
Flower bed Climbing frame			

Look carefully at your table. Which would be the best way for the tree to fall?

Think carefully. Should your decision just rest on the number of things in each column? Discuss your ideas with the group.

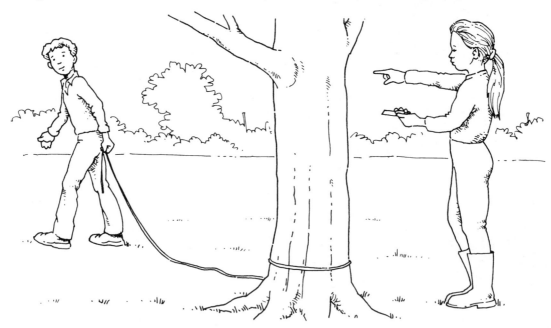

PHOTOCOPIABLE

Biggest and Smallest Challenge

Can you find the longest or shortest, the widest or narrowest, the heaviest or lightest ... ?

The lightest piece of litter

The heaviest stone

The thickest piece of wood

The shortest route to the pond

The widest flower bed

The narrowest gate

The longest wall in the school

Litter Bins Challenge

Find the best way to measure how much rubbish the litter bins hold.

Can you design a rubbish bin with two compartments?

One part is for biodegradable rubbish and the other part for non-biodegradable.

How can you find out which compartment needs to be bigger?

PHOTOCOPIABLE

Shape and Space in the School Grounds

As we handle three-dimensional objects and move about in our indoor and outdoor environments, part of everyday living involves the exploration of shape and space. Mainly through their senses of sight and touch children, from the moment of birth, build up a bank of spatial experience. Few parents realize that their children have had far more contact with geometry before they start school than they have had with number. Once in school children need to have their curiosity about the world of shape and space stimulated. They need to learn to speak the language of geometry so that they can give precise form to their questions and thoughts. They also need the understanding and the skills to represent their world by drawing diagrams, maps, plans and nets. Early attempts to represent shape and space on paper help to develop understanding.

The grounds of the school offer an abundance of spatial explorations which will complement the teaching of Attainment Target 4, Shape and Space, with real experience. The outdoor classroom can help to provide the necessary material and the following pages offer examples of suitable activities.

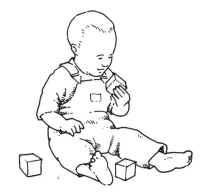

The school grounds provide abundant opportunities for exploring shape and space.

Looking at reflections in the pond can lead to a study of reflective symmetry.

Leaves are just one example of the variety of natural shapes to be found.

Using building blocks to copy the patterns in brickwork

Measuring angles outside helps to develop an understanding of geometry.

Shape and spatial work in the outdoor classroom   Key Stage 1

Strands	Pond	Animals	Pathways and Visitors	Allotment, Trees and Shrubs	Buildings	Conservation Area	Games and Activities	Weather
2D shape / 3D shape	What shape is the pond? Is it regular or irregular, curved or straight? Describe shapes around and in the pond (leaves, rocks, etc.). Which are regular shapes?	Identifying and naming shapes in the animal enclosures and houses. What are the best shapes for feeding bowls and drink containers? Why?	Look at: shapes of paving stones, tessellation of stones and slabs. Straight or curved pathways?	What shapes occur in nature? Look at 6 leaves, 6 flowers or 6 vegetables. Discuss straight and curved edges, regular and irregular shapes. Are there any angles?	Look at: shapes of bricks, stones, buildings, doors, windows, roof. Tessellation in brick and stone work.	Look at shapes that occur in nature. Look at leaves, petals, mini-beasts. Shape of birds' eggs.	Look at: circles in games, shapes in formal games. What is best shape for marbles, balls, hoops, etc.?	Look at shadows made by various 2D shapes. Look at shape of roof and angle of slope. Why does it slope? What problems do flat roofs have?
Location / Movement	Give instructions to walk around the pond. Describe a frog's journey across the pond using positional language, then more specific language, and compass bearings. Reflections leading to reflective symmetry.	Position of cages, animals, etc. 'The rabbit is on/behind the hutch.' Heighten perception of angles, straight lines, horizontals and verticals. Corners of pens – are there right angles?	Instructions for moving along pathways. Description of position in relation to pathways. Maps and instructions to visitors, including compass bearings and descriptions of rotational movements to find specific points.	Positions of plants, trees. Where does each grow best? Instructions for locating plants/rows in allotment. Position in relation to compass bearings (e.g. facing south). Symmetry of leaves, flowers and trees.	Position of doors and windows within walls. Are there vertical and horizontal lines, right angles in frames, walls, etc.? Where do windows face? When do they get sun? Are windows and doors in walls placed symmetrically? If not, what is the reason?	Language to describe position of habitats. Are there vertical and horizontal lines and right angles in nature? Which way do habitats face? Symmetry in leaves, flowers, mini-beasts.	Directions to play games. Positions in games or markings for games. Right angles in formal games. Large play equipment – vertical and sloping lines and the angles that result. Mirror-image games when children copy each other.	Where is it best to put a rain gauge? Why? Should drain pipes be horizontal and vertical or sloping? Why? Position of sun and direction of sunshine. Wind directions. Shadows – are they symmetrical? Do they accurately reflect? Mirror images.

Shape and spatial work in the outdoor classroom   Key Stage 2

Strands	Pond	Animals	Pathways and Visitors	Allotment, Trees and Shrubs	Buildings	Conservation Area	Games and Activities	Weather
2D shape	Design a pond using irregular and 2D shapes. Which do you prefer? Discuss lines and angles used.	Design animal enclosures and houses using knowledge of 2D or 3D shapes.	Design a pathway system around the school. Will it be straight or curved? What kind of corners will it have? Measure the angles of the corners.	What shapes are the canopies of the trees?	Make a model of all or part of your school building. What shapes have you used? What angles and lines have you used?	Look again at shape in nature and compare to manmade shapes.	Measure circumference of circles used in circle games. Plan out a formal games marking. How can you make sure all the lines are straight, the edges are parallel and the angles are right angles?	What shapes are shadows – irregular or regular?
3D shape	Possibly draw design on computer using turtle graphics.	Make a model of your design. Which is the best shape? Consider the angle of the roof. Measure and test several roof slopes.	Decide on the best shape of paving slabs. Draw shapes to test your ideas.	Design and make containers to pack fruit and vegetables into. Which shapes are best? Design a wheelbarrow. What shape should it be?	What angle do you think the slope of the roof is? Why?	Design a bird nesting box. What shape should it be? What shape should the entrance be? Make a bird table. Plan how the upright support will be perpendicular. What shapes will offer additional support?		Make a sundial, working out the angles between divisions. How long does it take the sun to move through a right angle?
Location	Draw a plan or map of pond using co-ordinates. Plan longest and shortest route to the pond.	Rotate the position of hutches, draw a plan to show as many possible positions as you can.	Draw a map for visitors, using co-ordinates to describe positions of main features.	Draw a plan of the planting in the allotment. Are all the rows straight?	Draw a plan of the school buildings using co-ordinates and showing which way each part faces.	Draw a map of the area, marking on habitats and nesting boxes.	Does a ball always bounce straight up or does it sometimes bounce at an angle? Find a way to test this.	Using a shadow stick, mark length of shadows against time. Use this to make a sundial.
Movement	Reflections in pond compared to mirror line reflections.	Draw a plan to show position of houses using co-ordinates. Which are best? Why?	Describe shortest/longest best route round the school. Give reasons.	What shape is the garden plot? How can the shape be most economically used? Do all rows need to be in same direction?		Rotate their positions to find out which is best.	Mark on a map where positions for a game could be.	

Position Challenge

over   underneath
around   in front of
between   next to
behind   on top of

Can you help the reception class to understand all the words at the top of the page?

Go outside, look around carefully and decide where in the playground they could safely carry out instructions which use those words. Then finish off all the sentences.

Stand between the ....
Go underneath the ....
Sit on top of the ....
Stand behind the ....
Stand in front of the ....
Go around the ....
Go over the ....
Stand next to the ....

There would be an awful mix up if all the children carried out one instruction at the same time. Can you plan a game which uses the instructions but makes sure that this doesn't happen?

When you have planned your game, take it along to the reception class teacher and ask politely whether the children could try it out. If the answer is yes, ask if you can watch. Do you think it helped the children to understand the words that we use to describe position in space?

PHOTOCOPIABLE

Symmetry Challenge

Can you answer questions like these about an object?

- Is it symmetrical?
- How do you know it is symmetrical?
- How many lines of symmetry does it have?
- Does it have mirror (reflective) symmetry?
- Does it have rotational symmetry?

In the chart below write down six things that you think might have symmetrical features. They must be things that you can find in the school grounds. Some of the objects should be natural and some manmade.

Now take your chart outside. Look carefully at each object you have chosen. If you made a drawing of the object, would you be able to put in any lines of symmetry? If you think you could, put ticks in the boxes.

Object	Lines of horizontal symmetry	Lines of vertical symmetry	Lines of rotational symmetry

PHOTOCOPIABLE

Shapes, Lines and Angles Challenge

Walk around the grounds of your school and try to complete this chart.

	Where can you see...?
A right angle	
An acute angle	
An obtuse angle	
An exterior angle	
An interior angle	
A vertical line	
A horizontal line	
Parallel lines	
A diagonal line	
A curved line	
An irregular shape	
A regular shape	
A hexagon	
An ovoid	

Can you make up a shape quiz for the rest of your class, based on what you have seen?

PHOTOCOPIABLE

Data Work in the School Grounds

Data handling is a vital part of everyday life. Children need to understand that data work is important and that knowledge and skills gained in mathematics lessons can and will need to be transferred to many other subjects.

There are four critical questions that children must learn to answer:

- What do I want or need to know?
- How am I going to get the information I need?
- How am I going to organize and represent the information?
- What did I find out?

What do I want or need to know?

Learning to ask the right questions at the right time is vital. Whenever children need to collect information we have to help them realize that they must be very clear in their own minds about what exactly it is they want to know. It is a thankless task to try to get children to ask questions about things they are not curious about. Well-developed school grounds where children are encouraged to take part in a wide variety of activities should provoke endless questioning. For example:

- How many species of birds visit our grounds?
- What is the largest number of snails we can find under a stone?
- What time of day are there most people out in the playground?

Data can be collected by direct observation.

How am I going to get the information I need?

The more varied their investigations, the greater the number of ways of obtaining information the children can explore.

1. Asking for opinions

- What is the best shape for a flower bed?
- Where shall we put the bird table?
- How can we keep the ground free of litter?

2. Drawing up questionnaires

- To find out what improvements the children would like in the grounds.
- To find out which is the most popular piece of play equipment.

Another method of data collection is to canvass people's opinions.

3. Counting and calculating

- Counting the number of bricks in a section of wall.
- Calculating the number of bricks in the whole length of the wall.

4. Measuring

- The height of a variety of flower species in the garden so that the average height can be found.

5. Making observations

- Observing the number of vehicles that pass the school in the first ten minutes of each hour of the school day.

6. Carrying out experiments

- Setting up a test to find out how far a seven-year-old can throw a ball.

How am I going to organize and represent the information?

Children need to learn to exercise choice and to select a way of representing information in the most easily accessible form. They will need to have had experience of:

1. Graphs: bar, column, line.
2. Charts: pie, pictograph.
3. Diagrams: Venn, Carroll, tree, flow.
4. Tables.

What did I find out?

Children also require the skills to interpret and make use of data. Practice will be needed in:

- Sifting data.
- Analysing and interpreting data.
- Drawing conclusions.
- Reporting findings.
- Justifying and generalizing.

The pages that follow provide a range of activities for data work in the school grounds.

A computer program can help with analysing data.

Once the data has been collected it needs to be represented in an accessible form.

Developing an understanding of data handling   Key Stage 1

	Pond	Animals	Pathways and Visitors	Allotment, Trees and Shrubs
Sorting	Pond creatures: species, legs, fins. Plant life: shape, colour of leaves, etc.	Sorting by: colour, covering, species, size, lays eggs, has babies, etc.	Sorting of traffic on pathways: visitors, children, to work, to play. Surface of pathways.	Sorting of crops: colour, stems, roots, fruits, flowers. Trees: leaf colour, shape, size.
Interpreting data: block graph, frequency tables, etc.	Collect and record data: growth of plants, change of tadpoles, variety of species, temperature.	Collect and record data: growth, amount of food eaten, varieties, colours, number of eggs laid.	Collect and record data: visitors to school, times, reasons they come, routes taken, traffic outside.	Collect and record data: types of crops, quantity total/per plant, weight, etc. Types of trees.
Sorting by two criteria (tree/Carroll/Venn diagrams)				

tails/legs

tadpoles fish frogs
legs legs legs
lilies
legs

tails tails

fur   brown

rabbit   guinea   Clara
         pig   the
                  hen

other hens
who are white

stones	bark	
grey stone	grass	
hard	not hard	

brown / not brown

turnip   beans
      carrot   tomato
green   green
      not green   not green

underground   not underground

All the data possibilities can be used on a data base or for more complex statistical diagrams.

	Pond	Animals	Pathways and Visitors	Allotment, Trees and Shrubs
Probability	It is certain that some tadpoles will become frogs. It is impossible they will become fish. It is uncertain how many will change.	It is certain that rabbits have baby rabbits. It is impossible for hens to make burrows. It is uncertain how many eggs will be laid this week.	It is certain that someone will walk on this path today. It is uncertain how many people will come today.	It is certain that a plant will not grow without water. It is impossible to grow pears on an apple tree. It is uncertain how many potatoes will grow.
Is it likely that ...	frogs will fly?	... rabbits will eat carrots?	... more than 4 visitors will come?	.... this plant will have only 2 pods?

Buildings	Conservation Area	Games and Activities	Weather
Sorting of building materials. Uses of buildings, number of windows or doors in a wall.	Sorting mini-beasts into number of legs, colour, etc. Sorting plant life, bird life	Sorting balls, bean bags, hoops, bats into size, colour, etc. Sorting wheeled toys into 2 wheels, 3 wheels, etc.	Sorting days into sunny, wet, cloudy, hot, cold, etc.
Collect and record data: building materials, number of windows and doors, direction they face.	Collect and record: numbers, characteristics of species, habitats. Bird watching. Changes by season.	Collect and record data: how far you can run/jump/throw; how quickly you can run/score 10 goals.	Collect and record data: rainfall, sunlight hours, wind speed, temperature.

Buildings	Conservation Area	Games and Activities	Weather
It is certain that the window will break if a brick hits it. It is impossible for a giraffe to fit through the door.	It is certain that there will be some woodlice under the log. It is impossible that we will find a snail as big as a cat. It is uncertain how many birds will visit today.	It is certain that someone will run across the playground. It is impossible that anyone will swim across. It is uncertain how many children will choose to go on the slide.	It is certain that it will get dark tonight. It is impossible that there will be heavy snow in July. It is uncertain if it will be sunny next week.
... the school will disappear?	... the spider will have 8 legs?	... someone will fall over?	... the sun will come out?

Developing an understanding of data handling   Key Stage 2

	Pond	Animals	Pathways and Visitors	Allotment, Trees and Shrubs	Buildings	Conservation Area	Games and Activities	Weather
Interrogate a database / **Draw conclusions from a database**	Use a database to find out which creatures swim. Decide on the best plants for height.	Use a database to choose bedding for each kind of animal.	Use a database to decide on a path to the most popular areas.	Use a database to plan planting of trees and shrubs for variety of heights.	Use a database to decide which entrance is used most and needs biggest door mat.	Use a database to decide on habitats different mini-beasts like: dark/light, wet/dry, etc.	Use simple data to keep scores of various games and activities. Draw up tables.	Use a database to find out if some months are wetter than others.
Conduct a survey on an issue of choice	Collect information on all the creatures in the pond.	Collect information about daily habits of animals.	Collect information on people who visit our school.	Survey all the trees and shrubs. Which ones produce fruit? Any other uses?	Survey all the rooms in the school, their size and uses. Could any be used for a new library?	Design and use a habitat recorder for an ecological survey of the area.	Make a survey of what children like to play outside and make a rota using the results.	Make a survey of weather over a term.
Devise and use an observation sheet to collect data	Count creatures in sample scoops. Decide on dominant species.	Decide on times they should be fed.	Decide which routes are most popular.	Plan any additions.				Decide on likelihood of sun for future events.
Use mean and range of a set of data	Mean and range of contents of 2 samples from pond.	Mean and range of money spent on food for hens compared to rabbits.	Mean and range of visitors to school a.m. and p.m. over a week.	Mean and range: compare the yield of 2 fruit bushes.	Mean and range of people using 2 entrances to the school.	Mean and range: compare woodlice in 2 habitats.	Mean and range: compare scores of 2 teams, but different number of games.	Mean and range: compare sunshine in May and June.
Interpret statistical diagrams	Interpret a pie chart of creatures living in pond.	Read a timetable telling time and weight of food.	Compare charts showing frequency/number of visitors.	Interpret a pie chart comparing species of trees and shrubs.	Read and understand a timetable for the use of the school hall.	Understand a frequency chart of bird species visiting table.	Read a chart that shows how fast each child runs round the field.	Read a pie chart that records types of weather over a month.
Estimate probability and use an appropriate method of estimating	Estimate with reasons the likelihood of picking up a frog in a scoop from the pond.	Estimate probability that hens will lay 3 eggs a day by doing a survey of egg laying.	If we are expecting 5 visitors at 9 o'clock the chance of any arriving first is 1:5.	4 gooseberry bushes will not all yield the same. Consider ways of estimating their probable yields.	Estimate the likelihood of someone slipping on a wet corridor floor. What should we do?	Decide that an estimate of probability of woodlice and slugs in each habitat can be made by doing a survey.	The chance of winning a game is not necessarily 1/3 win/lose/draw. Other ways of estimating outcome?	Estimate with reasons the likelihood of rain tomorrow.

Skipping Challenge

Carry out a skipping survey.

Here are some questions to answer and some things to do which will help your investigation.

1. How many children in our school can skip using a rope?
2. Is this more or less than half of the school population?
3. Are there any children in our highest age group who can't skip?
4. Do girls and boys both enjoy skipping?
5. Can all the teachers skip?

Choose a group of ten children.

Ask each one of them to skip for as long as they can until they are tired.
Count how many times the rope passes under their feet and then record it.
Draw a bar graph to show their scores.
Write as many facts as you can from the information that the graph gives you.

Coming and Going Challenge

Find out as much as you can about the number of people who use the different entrances and exits to the school grounds.

Here are some questions to help your investigation.

1. Which is the most used entrance to the school grounds?
2. Which is the most used entrance to the building?
3. Do most people who visit the school enter and leave by the same gate and door?

Present the data you collect in two different ways. Then decide which method is the easiest to get information from.

What use could you make of the information you obtained?

PHOTOCOPIABLE

Games Outside Challenge

Can you devise and conduct a survey during playtimes and the lunch hour to discover how many different kinds of games are being played and which are the most popular?

Here are some headings to get you started. Perhaps you can think of others to add to the list.

Ring games
Chase games
Ball games
'Let's pretend' games

See if you can find out:

1. Which game is the most popular with each of the year groups that we have in school?
2. What size of group do most children play in?
3. Are there more single-sex groups or more mixed groups?
4. Do most people stick to just one game at playtime or do they play two or three different ones? Is it the same at lunchtime?

Think carefully about how you will present the information you obtain. Is there a computer program which might help you?

A Summer's Day of Mathematics Outside

9.30 a.m. ...

Lines and planes were being investigated by a class of eleven-year-olds and the words 'perpendicular', 'parallel', 'horizontal' and 'vertical' had been savoured and explored for some days. The children's understanding of the concepts was still vague and more experience was needed to increase their understanding. Their teacher suggested to the student on teaching practice who was working with them that they might be fascinated by a search for examples in the school grounds. Now all twenty-eight of them were outside, armed with clipboards, pencils, plumb-lines and home-made spirit-levels, to see if they could find examples of these four types of line in both the natural and the artificial environments.

The wall at the front of the school and the fence at the back offered examples of all four types of line and the fence raised questions which led to the word 'oblique' being introduced. The children knew that a quarter turn was called a right angle and they had used a set square in the classroom. Miriam asked if she could go back to the classroom to collect one in order to check some of the corners she was exploring in her quest for the perpendicular. This prompted several other children to ask to get one too. One of the best assessment of understanding techniques which teachers have at their disposal is to be constantly on the look-out for transference of knowledge and skills from one situation to another. Miriam was obviously well on her way to a grasp of the relationship between the horizontal and the perpendicular which results in a right angle.

The children found parallel lines as they looked at the courses in the bricks, the wooden planking of the shed and in the relationship between the two edges of a path. Vertical and horizontal they found in doors and gates, drainpipes and guttering, the markings for netball courts and hundred squares. A particular excitement was caused by the lines of shadows cast on the walls and the ground.

Investigating lines and planes in the school grounds

The children were really engrossed in the 'line hunt' when they moved from the built to the natural environment of the school. What had trees, shrubs and plants to offer to the growing list of examples? Suddenly the word 'almost' was in the air: 'That branch is almost parallel to that one', 'That lateral stem is almost at a right angle to the main stem'. Would they find any true examples or not? Everywhere there seemed to be pairs of children furiously debating whether they had found a true example of the definition of horizontal, parallel, perpendicular or vertical, or not. The search caused them to exclaim over shafts of light and discuss the horizontal plane of the surface of water. Most important, it brought them up against the degree of 'exactness' that they were prepared to accept to fulfil their criteria. The children were experiencing what it is to talk and behave as mathematicians.

10 a.m. ...

With great excitement a class of five-year-olds came into the garden with their teacher. Today they were going to dig up a potato. It was not just any old potato, but their own potato and it had the name of 'Spud'.

Some months ago their headteacher had found a forgotten sack of potatoes in her garage and had brought it into school for the children to see. As they looked down into the sack, the children saw what appeared to be a small forest becoming established. They were challenged to research the phenomenon. Each class was given a potato with the instruction to plant it in the allotment and monitor its growth.

In the reception classroom the potato was named 'Spud'. Then the planting of the potato was discussed. A book on vegetable gardening was found in the library and their teacher read the planting instructions to the class. The burning question was how big a hole was needed for planting. As discussion progressed, the need for refinement of spatial language became obvious and soon the words 'wide' and 'deep' occurred. The book said that potatoes take about seventeen weeks to grow. How many days, then would they have to wait for their potato, 'Spud', to grow? Guesses were recorded and a chart designed to record the number of days between planting and harvest. What else would they like to find out about? Suggestions came thick and fast...

A decision was made that once Spud was planted, her rate of growth should be measured every Monday. A final question concerned what care Spud would need to help her grow into a healthy plant. If it didn't rain the plant would need watering. How much water? How often? Mathematics was rearing its head yet again. Another chart was designed, this time to record rainfall. The rule alongside the chart was clear ...

Three days without rain – Spud must be watered.

With due ceremony Spud was planted. A record of the date and time was made in the potato's 'This was your life' book. Each time more than three days passed without rain, Spud was given two cans of water. Each Monday Spud's height was marked in scarlet on a cane kept specially for the purpose. Language flowed during the measuring sessions ...

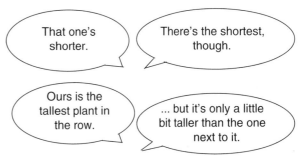

... and the children learnt the relative language of measurement.

As the weeks passed the potato flowered. Finally, the digging up day arrived. It was time for some estimation. How many small potatoes would there be? How far down would they have to dig to find all the small potatoes? How long would it take them to harvest all the small potatoes?

Spud was dug up and eighteen small potatoes were extracted from the earth between her roots. Never was counting so carefully done. The harvest was spread out on the grass and sorting by size took place immediately, causing lively debate and much bandying of words such as 'big, bigger, biggest', 'small, smaller, smallest', not to mention 'whopper' and 'tiny'. Size was compared with weight. Did the biggest one feel the heaviest?

Then came the volume work. Would all the potatoes fit into the box the children had brought out with them? Yes, they'd been nothing if not optimistic, there was room to

The potato harvest

spare. Triumphantly the potatoes were carried back to the classroom.

The next problem was what to do with the potatoes now that they had them! The solution seemed obvious – eat them. How many different ways of cooking potatoes could they think of? The options were listed and a survey undertaken of the children's favourite way of eating potatoes. They painted seven cardboard plates with pictures of differently cooked potatoes. These were stuck in a row along the top of a piece of card. The children then drew pictures of their own faces on card and mapped them on to their favourite way of eating potato. The results were ten for chips, eight for mashed, four for baked, three for roasted, four for boiled. Not one chose waffled. In this way the data connected with the survey was recorded.

Spud's offspring were compared with other types of potato bought from the local supermarket by their teacher. The fact that different types of potato lend themselves to cooking in different ways was discussed at length.

The children accepted their teacher's advice that Spud's potatoes were really most suitable for boiling. So wonderful new potatoes were solemnly boiled and dressed with parsley and butter, to be shared out and eaten by the children.

Finally, an epitaph was written for Spud's book.

11 a.m. ...

Half a dozen seven-year-olds, accompanied by a parent helper, made their way to the conservation area. In a tray they carried some sticks, a ball of string and a pair of scissors. Each child marked out an area 5 feet long and 2 feet wide (in body measurements, not imperial).

Their next task was to see how many different kinds of grasses they could find in their patch. They drew the different species and then returned to their classroom.

How many kinds of grasses are there in our marked-out area?

A few days earlier a discussion about 'average numbers' had taken place. To explore this term, it was decided to collate and compare one another's findings about the numbers of species of grasses in the 5 by 2 patches. The range of results was discussed and a matrix designed to show the six results.

	1	2	3	4	5	6
Paul					✓	
Kate						✓
Kim			✓			
Rajip			✓			
Ann					✓	
Sue		✓				

Examination of the results, together with more explanation from their teacher about the meaning of the term, led the children to predict that the average would be five. It was time to use the calculators. The children were given the method:

'Add the six different results together and then divide the total by the number of children who collected them.'

The result – four – provoked a great deal of talk. How could that be the answer? Was it the right answer?

It would be foolish to claim that as a result of this work the children had gained an understanding of the mathematical term 'average'. What they did gain was a little experience which, when accompanied by further experiences, would permit sound concept development to take place.

2 p.m. ...

Mrs Dyer brought her class of six-year-olds outside to pick raspberries. A standard had been set for the shade of red which would indicate that the fruit was ripe enough for picking. The unit of measurement to be used was a 'cupful'. Two cupfuls would go into a plastic bag. A timer was set to 'ping' at ten minutes, the time allowed for picking.

Time was up and the children returned to the classroom to count the number of bags from the day's harvest. The total available for sale to parents at home time was nine.

How much should be charged for the raspberries? If they were sold at 10p a bag, how much would that be altogether? A tin of real coins was collected from the office, and ten pennies were laid out beside each bag of fruit. What a lot of counting to do! Did the coins have to be counted in ones or was there another way of doing it? Other coins were examined: 2p, 5p, 10p, 20p and 50p coins were laid out on the table and named. Any ideas?

Picking raspberries in the school garden

With excitement, Ian remembered previous work done on exchanging 1p coins for larger denominations. He grabbed a 10p piece and suggested changing it for the ten coins by the first bag of raspberries. This was done. Was it going to help them count? You bet it was! This class had done a lot of counting in tens. All the groups of pennies were exchanged for 10p coins and then counting began.

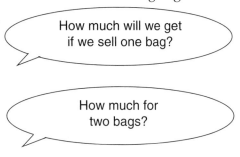

> How much will we get if we sell one bag?

> How much for two bags?

The investigation was recorded in table form. A little light multiplication, then economics reared its head! If more money were charged per bag, more profit would be made. Was the price set for the raspberries cheap or dear? How much was the grocer across the road charging?

Scouts were sent to find out. The punnets were 75p each and appeared to hold about the same amount of raspberries as the bags. The difference between the shop's price and the children's was no less than 65p! What was to be done about it? Were they to offer the bargain of the year, or should they raise the price?

In the end a price of 25p per bag was settled on, and that evening the raspberries were put on sale and quickly bought. The grand total of £2.25 was banked in the gardening fund. We are saving up for a new mulberry tree to replace the old one lost in the drought.

2.30 p.m. ...

Some five-year-olds came out into the garden with their classroom assistant. They had with them the five minute sand timer; their teacher had asked them to see how long a daisy chain they could make in that time.

The children worked individually. The skill of chain making had been diligently acquired with the help of patient dinner supervisors throughout the summer. Once back in the classroom, the children compared the lengths of their chains. The words 'long, longer, longest, short, shorter, shortest' were all used. An estimation was made of how far the chain might stretch if all the pieces were joined together. This was done and the children were excited to find that it stretched across the classroom.

David realized that the room was longer than it was wide. The children wondered how many more daisies they would have to pick to stretch that far, and immediately wanted to attempt it. Their teacher said that it would take too long to complete that before going home time. The discussion was taking a very mathematical turn. In the end it was decided that the whole class would pick daisies at playtime the next day and make a chain as long as the length of the room.

They did it!

The day after that it rained so the children couldn't go into the garden. But their teacher used the experience with the daisies as a starting point for some algebra work. She drew them a picture of a mathematician's garden where the daisies were only allowed to grow according to a very strict rule. The children were challenged to discover the pattern of the sequence.

Throughout the day and the day after ...

Fixed to an outside wall of the school were two netball goals. Mr Smith's class of ten-year-olds had been exploring averages and their teacher had challenged them to use the rings for some of the practical work. What would be the average number of goals scored per class member out of ten shots, first from 1 metre away, and secondly from 2 metres away?

A great deal of class discussion followed to allow decisions to be taken about appropriate procedures and recording methods. How long would it take to get through the whole class, each having twenty shots at goal? Would they get through it in one day or would they need two? The answer was to find out how long it would take one child to do it first! Guesses varied wildly from two minutes to a quarter of an hour. This was no basis for drawing up a timetable. Mr Smith grinned when Sarah said, 'We need to know the average time taken.'

What else did they need to make decisions about? Shaun said it was important to measure and mark the 1 metre and the 2 metre spots where the shooters had to stand.

Parvinda thought a decision should be made about how the scores were to be recorded and how to ensure that everybody had ten shots from each distance. In the end one group of four children was delegated to decide on and set up the recording procedures for the next day, while Claire and Elaine had the job of measuring out and deciding how to mark the shooting positions. When Gulzar, Sue, Sundeep and Ian had devised shot tallying and result recording procedures, then Martin was to go out with six children, a stopwatch and a netball and time them, each taking twenty shots, and also try out the tallying and recording.

Claire and Elaine took a metre stick and went outside to try to find the best way of marking the two shooting positions. Their first idea was to use rounders base posts, but this raised the problem of whether the shooters should stand behind, in front of or at the side of the post and the greater problem of the posts being moved when people stood alongside them. What appeared to be needed was a mark on the ground. Chalk would get rubbed out. A masking tape cross was finally accepted as satisfactory.

Next it was Martin's turn to choose three

Scoring netball goals is an enjoyable way of exploring averages.

boys and three girls and time each of them taking twenty shots at goal. Back in the classroom Mr Smith helped Martin to find the average time and then gave him and Nicola the task of drawing up a timetable for the next day. Just before lunch Martin was required to explain to his classmates how he'd found the average time taken – five minutes – and how he and Nicola had then drawn up a timetable. Their explanation of the amount of time they'd allowed for change-over between each pair was most impressive.

The next day the children went to the playground in groups of four. Child A took ten shots at goal from 1 metre. Child B tallied the number of shots taken and recorded the goals scored. Roles were then reversed. Next they repeated the sequence from the 2 metre distance. Back in the classroom each child entered their results on a matrix. Once every result had been entered, Mr Smith reminded his class of the method of finding an average. Using their calculators, every child then had a go at getting a result. It turned out to be three goals at 1 metre and one at 2 metres.

The task had a high motivation level and a lot of interest was aroused. Other questions were raised. Why was the average so low when some of the children were good at shooting? If everyone got in a lot of practice in a week could they raise the average number of goals scored or would it take longer than that?

At the end of the task the class were asked to identify all the mathematical work they had been engaged in. The list was quite impressive: data recording and analysis, measuring distance and time, the drawing up and reading of timetables, and of course the work that was the primary objective of the exercise, a deepening of their understanding of the term 'average'.

A Summer's Day of Mathematics Outside
The activities described relate to the following National Curriculum Attainment Targets

AT1 Using and Applying
Using materials for a practical task
Talking about their work and asking questions
Making predictions based on experience
Selecting the materials and the mathematics to use for a practical task
Describing work and checking results

AT2 Number
Understanding the language associated with number, e.g. 'the same'
Making a sensible estimate
Solving whole number problems involving addition and subtraction, including money
Using non-standard measures
Using decimal notation in recording money
Recognising and understanding simple percentages

AT4 Shape and Space
Recognising types of movement
Understand angle as a measurement of turn

AT5 Handling Data
Designing a data collection sheet
Constructing frequency tables and block graphs
Interpreting charts
Understanding 'fair and unfair'
Specifying an issue for which data is needed
Use of variables
Understanding, calculating and using the mean of a set of data

Resources

USEFUL ORGANIZATIONS

All of these organizations produce a range of resources that will help in developing school grounds.

British Trust for Conservation Volunteers
36 St Mary's Street
Wallingford
Oxon OX10 0EJ

Centre for Alternative Technology
Llwyngwern Quarry
Machynlleth
Powys SY20 9AZ

Common Ground
c/o London Ecology Centre
45 Sheldon Street
London WC2 9HJ

Council for Environmental Education School
  of Education
University of Reading
Reading
Berkshire RG1 5AQ

Friends of the Earth
26-28 Underwood Street
London N1 7JQ

Learning through Landscapes
Third Floor, Southside Offices
The Law Courts
Winchester
Hants SO23 9DL

National Association for Environmental
  Education
Wolverhampton Polytechnic
Walsall Campus
Gorway
Walsall
West Midlands WS1 3BD

National Association for Urban Studies
Lewis Cohen Urban Studies Centre
University of Brighton
68 Grand Parade
Brighton BN2 2JY

National Children's Play and Recreation Unit
359-361 Euston Road
London NW1 3AL

Tidy Britain Group
The Pier
Wigan WN3 4EX

Tree Council
35 Belgrave Square
London SW1X 8QN

WATCH/Royal Society for
  Nature Conservation
The Green
Witham Park
Waterside South
Lincoln LN5 7JR

World Wide Fund for Nature
Panda House
Weyside Park
Godalming
Surrey GU7 1XR

A variety of useful charts are available from
Pictorial Charts Education Trust
27 Kirchen Road
London W13 0UD

BIBLIOGRAPHY

Mathematics Counts, the report of the Cockcroft Committee (H.M.S.O.). It states unequivocally that the principal reason for teaching mathematics to all children is that it is a powerful means of communication which is concise and unambiguous.

Primary Mathematics Today, E.M. Williams and Hilary Shuard (Longman). The reference book on the teaching of mathematics which no school can afford to be without. The late Hilary Shuard was one of our country's finest mathematical educators.

Mathematics for Young Children, Marion H. Bird (Routledge). The author demonstrates the ability of children to take their own initiative within mathematics.

Children and Number, Martin Hughes (Basil Blackwell), stresses the importance of building links between children's formal and informal understanding of number.

Children's Minds, Margaret Donaldson (Fontana), encourages teachers continually to examine the ways in which children learn.

Maths in the environment

Active Maths: Primary Maths from the Environment (World Wide Fund for Nature, 1991, available from Southgate Publishers)

Esso Schoolwatch pack (Learning through Landscapes, 1992)

Children First: A Cross-curricular Approach to Key Stage One of the National Curriculum (Southgate Publishers, 1990-91) A series of four books containing a total of twelve topics covering the core and foundation subjects and relating to children's everyday experiences.